SMART WORDS
—— READER ——

Fossils

Judith Bauer Stamper
Vicky Willows

SCHOLASTIC INC.

What are SMART WORDS?

Smart Words are frequently used words that are critical to understanding concepts taught in the classroom. The more Smart Words a child knows, the more easily he or she will grasp important curriculum concepts. Smart Words readers introduce these key words in a fun and motivational format while developing important literacy skills. Each new word is highlighted, defined in context, and reviewed. Engaging activities at the end of each chapter allow readers to practice the words they have learned.

ISBN 978-0-545-28546-9

Packaged by Q2AMedia

Copyright © 2010 by Scholastic Inc.

Photo credits: t= top, b= bottom, l= left, r= right

Cover Page: Tonnyx/Dreamstime, Zuleima/Shutterstock.
Title Page: John Cancalosi/Photolibrary.
Content Page: Photolibrary.

6: Charlie Hutton/Shutterstock; 7: Alexal/Shutterstock; 6-7: Heiko Grossmann/ Istockphoto; 8: John Cancalosi/Photolibrary; 9: Eremin Sergey/Shutterstock; 10: Anton Foltin/Dreamstime; 11: Michael Ledray/Shutterstock; 12: Mike Brake/ Bigstock; 13: Stephen J Krasemann/Photolibrary; 14: Markrhiggins/Shutterstock; 15: George Burba/Shutterstock; 17t: Triff/Shutterstock; 17c: Regien Paassen/ Shutterstock; 17b: Abutyrin/Shutterstock; 18: Darryl Brooks/Dreamstime; 19: Digital Studio/Shutterstock; 20: Falk Kienas/Shutterstock; 21: UPPA/Photoshot; 22: Doug Lee/Photolibrary; 23t: Martin Maun/Shutterstock; 23b: Russell Shively/Shutterstock; 24-25: MaxPhoto/Shutterstock; 26: Rich Koele/Shutterstock; 27: Kjersti Wasiak/ Bigstock; 28: Arpad Benedek/Istockphoto; 29: Russell Shively/Shutterstock; 30-31t: Tom Grundy/Shutterstock; 30-31b: Markrhiggins/Shutterstock.

Q2AMedia Art Bank: 4-5, 16, 25.

25 24 23 22 21   14 15/0

Printed in the U.S.A.   40
First printing, September 2010

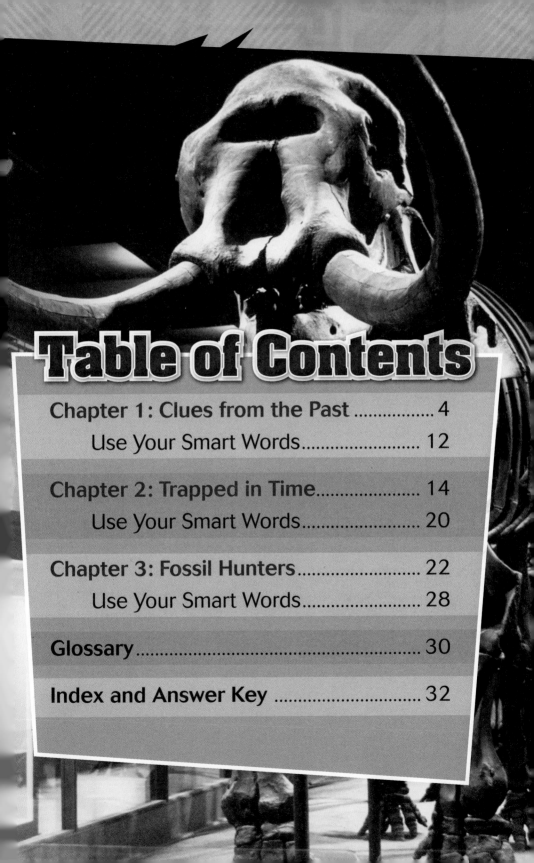

Table of Contents

Chapter 1

Clues from the Past

A *Tyrannosaurus rex*, also known as *T. rex*, opens his huge jaws. His fifty, long, dagger-like teeth sink into the tasty *Triceratops* he is having for dinner. As the *T. rex* dines, winged reptiles flap across the sky. Off in the thick forest of ferns, a herd of hadrosaurs are using their tough beaks and numerous teeth to grind up a dinner of plants.

This is not a scene from a book or movie. It is a story told by Earth's **fossils**. A fossil is any **evidence** or remains of an organism that once lived on Earth. Fossils are our clues to the past.

For example, *T. rex* lived 65 to 85 million years ago. It is now **extinct**, gone forever from the Earth. But its story, including how it lived and what it ate, remains forever in the fossils it left behind.

SMART WORDS

fossil   any evidence or remains of an organism that once lived on Earth

evidence   any sign or indication that proves something

extinct   when all animals or plants of a certain type die and none are left

Hard Parts and Soft Parts

When most people think of fossils, they think of old bones. But fossils are not only bones. They include other evidence as well. For example, think about other hard parts, like teeth or eggs. Yes, they are fossils, too!

The hard parts of animals do not decay, or rot away, as quickly as the soft parts. They may be **preserved** in their original state. When scientists put together all the bones and teeth, they can get a good picture of what each animal looked like.

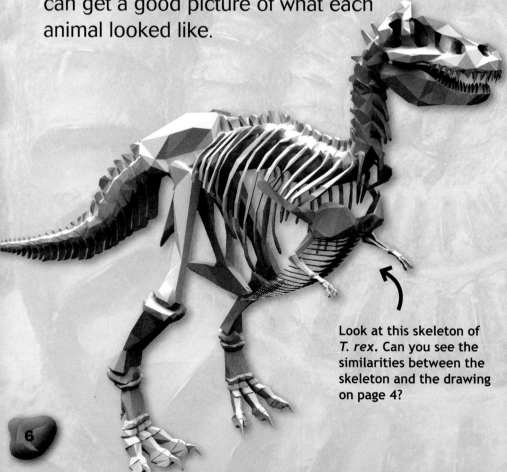

Look at this skeleton of *T. rex*. Can you see the similarities between the skeleton and the drawing on page 4?

Animal eggs tell scientists how organisms **reproduced**, or made more of themselves. Fossils of dinosaur eggs have been found with entire skeletons of babies inside! This tells scientists that dinosaurs laid eggs just like most modern reptiles.

Teeth can tell a lot about what an animal ate. Animals that eat both meat and plants have four front center teeth for biting. On either side are pointed teeth used for tearing and shredding meat. Back teeth are flat for grinding.

SMART WORDS

preserve   to protect something so that it stays in its original state

reproduce   to make more of one's own kind

Earth's story would not be complete without plants and animals that have no hard parts! But, how are these fossils made?

Plants like ferns leave behind fossils, too. Dead plants are often buried in sand or mud. Over time, the sand and mud turn into rock, and the plant slowly disappears. However, an **imprint**, or impression, is left behind as a fossil in the rock.

Animals leave imprints, as well. Soft, thin parts of their bodies, such as skin or feathers, may leave an impression before decaying.

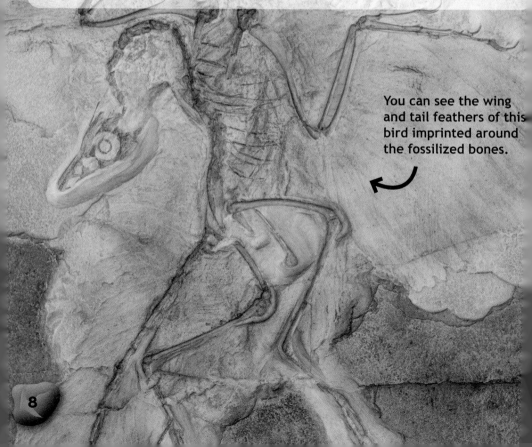

You can see the wing and tail feathers of this bird imprinted around the fossilized bones.

Other types of fossils are formed when an organism is buried in mud or sand that becomes rock.

A 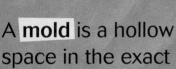 **mold** is a hollow space in the exact shape of the organism. In nature, a mold forms when mud or sand hardens around a buried plant or animal. The organism decays, and only the space it occupied is left. If that space fills with minerals, and the minerals harden, this forms a **cast**. The cast is in the exact shape of the organism that was buried there.

SMART WORDS

imprint an impression left by a thin object in sand or mud that hardens into rock

mold a hollow space in the exact shape of the original organism

cast a fossil formed when sand, mud, or minerals harden inside a mold

Trace Fossils

Remember the *T. rex* you read about? Its feet were 3.3 feet (1 meter) long. But its footprints were only 1.55 feet (.47 meter) long. When scientists put this evidence together, they figured out that *T. rex* walked on its toes!

Footprints, or trackways, are an example of **trace fossils**. These are marks or signs that an animal has left behind. Trace fossils provide a lot of information about an animal. For example, footprints tell us if the animal walked on two legs or four.

Other kinds of trace fossils may be left by soft-bodied animals, such as worms. Worms leave behind burrows or tunnels in the soil where they once lived.

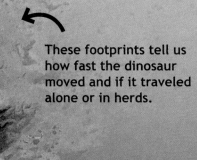

These footprints tell us how fast the dinosaur moved and if it traveled alone or in herds.

Trace fossils also give us clues about what ancient animals ate. For example, meat-eaters, like saber-tooth tigers, left teeth marks in the bones of their victims.

These saber-toothed tiger teeth very likely left scratch marks on the bones of the tiger's victims.

Fossilized scat (a cool word for poop) can tell us what an animal ate. Remember the *Triceratops* the *T. rex* was having for dinner? In a day or two, bits of body parts would have been dropped in the scat of the *T. rex*. If preserved, the scat would tell scientists millions of years later what was on the menu!

SMART WORD

trace fossil a visible mark or sign of animal activity

Match each clue with the correct Smart Word.

> trace fossil / evidence / preserve / imprint
>
> mold   extinct   reproduce   cast   fossil

1. an impression left by a thin object in sand or mud that hardens into rock

2. a visible mark or sign of animal activity

3. any evidence or remains of an organism that once lived on Earth

4. a fossil that forms when sand, mud, or minerals harden inside a mold

5. a hollow space with the imprint of a plant or animal

6. when all animals or plants of a certain type die and none are left

7. to protect something so that it stays in its original state

8. any sign or indication that proves something

9. to make more of one's own kind

Answers on page 32

Talk Like a Scientist

Use Smart Words to describe a fossil you read about. Tell what it is, and how it formed.

SMART FACTS

Record Breaker!

How big are dinosaur eggs? The biggest ever found are one foot long and shaped like footballs.

How Strange!

Also known as a "Water Demon," the huge *Plesiosaur* lived 65 to 220 million years ago. It was described as having "the head of a lizard, teeth of a crocodile, and a body resembling a serpent."

That's Amazing!

Fossils of ocean organisms have been found in parts of the United States, including Nebraska, Kansas, Indiana, Pennsylvania, and New York. This means these areas were once covered by shallow seas!

Chapter 2

TRAPPED IN TIME

Most plants and animals never become fossils. They are eaten or their remains decay very quickly. However, a quick burial protects the remains and slows down decay.

Some dead animals were quickly covered by **sediment**, small pieces of sand, mud, and rock. Over time, more layers of sediment piled on top of the remains. Each new layer quite possibly held the remains of other organisms. Over time, the layers of sediment turned into **sedimentary rock**.

Most fossils are found in sedimentary rock.

What happened next was really incredible!

Rainwater containing **minerals** seeped through the layers of sediment, reaching the buried bones. It entered small holes in the bones. When the water disappeared, the minerals were left. The bones turned to stone. This process is called **petrification**.

Bones are not the only things that can be petrified. Minerals can also seep into dead trees. Slowly, the minerals replace the wood. The petrified wood looks exactly like the original tree. But it is hard rock.

These trees in Petrified Forest National Park are hard as rock.

SMART WORDS

sediment small pieces of sand, mud, pebbles, and the remains of dead organisms

sedimentary rock rock formed by layers of sediment in the ground being pressed together

mineral a nonliving solid that occurs in nature

petrification the process in which an animal or plant turns to stone

Follow along in the diagram to see how one animal was buried and its bones became petrified.

How a Fossil Forms

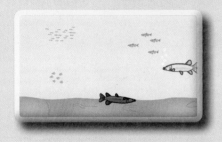

1. A dead fish sinks to the bottom of the ocean. The soft parts of its body begin to rot.

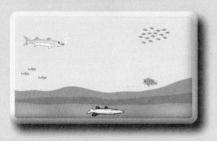

2. Layers of sediment cover the skeleton. Minerals in the water seep into the bones. Over time, the bones turn to stone.

3. More sediment covers the fish. The new layers squeeze the sediment together into sedimentary rock.

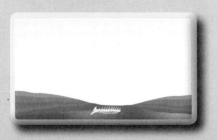

4. After millions of years, the Earth moves and pushes up the rock. The hidden fossil is found.

From Fossils to Fuels

You may be surprised to learn that the remains of some ancient plants and animals turned into the **fossil fuels** that run your television or computer today!

All energy on Earth comes from the sun. Green plants and some ocean-dwelling creatures change energy from the sun into food. Some of the energy is stored in the plants' or animals' bodies. When they die, that energy is buried with them.

Over millions of years, the remains of the plants and animals were buried deeper and deeper in layers of sediment. Heat and pressure changed the remains into fossil fuel. Fossil fuels are coal, oil, and natural gas. They are used today to produce electricity.

SMART WoRD

fossil fuel   fuel formed from the remains of ancient plants and animals

Frozen Solid

It is extremely rare to find a fossil of a complete organism, including its soft parts like skin and organs. But, it does happen.

If you want to preserve some kinds of food, you put them in the freezer. Earth has a gigantic freezer – the great sheets of ice around the North Pole. Scientists have found now-extinct giant woolly mammoths and furry rhinoceroses perfectly preserved in ice!

These animals were so well preserved that animals in the area tried to eat the 10,000-year-old flesh when it thawed!

Woolly mammals roamed the Earth some 10,000 years ago.

Sticky Situations

Thousands of fossils are buried in **tar pits**. These sticky pools of black tar trapped animals. Eventually, they would sink to the bottom of the tar pit. Although most fossils in tar pits are bones, some complete animals have been perfectly preserved.

Other animals were preserved in another kind of sticky substance called sap. Sap is made by certain types of evergreen trees. When it hardens, it forms a hard material called **amber**. If an insect crawled or flew into the sap, it would be trapped in amber forever.

This insect has been trapped in sticky sap.

SMART WORDS

tar pit   a pool of black, sticky tar

amber   a hard substance made from the hardened sap of some evergreen trees

Use your SMART WORDS

Read each clue. Choose the Smart Word it describes.

| sediment | mineral | amber | tar pit |
| sedimentary rock | petrification | fossil fuel |

1. a hard substance formed from tree sap
2. a rock formed by layers of sediment in the ground being pressed together
3. the process in which an animal or plant turns to stone
4. a pool of black, sticky tar
5. fuel formed from the remains of ancient plants and animals
6. nonliving solid that occurs in nature
7. small pieces of sand, mud, pebbles, and the dead remains of organisms

Answers on page 32

Talk Like a Scientist

Look at the photo. How did this fossil form? Use Smart Words to talk about it.

SMART FACTS

That's Amazing!

Mosquitoes trapped in amber are perfect fossils. In fact, some still contain their victim's blood!

Incredible Find!

Leonardo is a mummified 77-million-year-old dinosaur. Although not wrapped in linen cloth like Egyptian mummies, Leonardo is considered a mummy since his soft parts have been preserved by nature. Even his stomach contents have been preserved. Before he died, the 3–4-year-old dinosaur had a meal of ferns and conifers.

Did You Know?

In 1997, a nine-year-old boy found a woolly mammoth preserved in ice in Siberia. Mammoths roamed the Earth during the last Ice Age. They were huge animals that looked like hairy elephants.

A baby woolly mammoth that was preserved in ice.

Chapter 3

Fossil Hunters

It's impossible to say when the first fossil was found, or even where. Long ago, in China, fossils were thought to be the bones of dragons. It was not until the early 1800s that a dinosaur fossil was found and someone actually realized what it was! This was the beginning of the science of **paleontology**, or the study of fossils.

Paleontologists are scientists who collect and study fossils. They use the **fossil record** to learn about organisms that existed throughout Earth's history. They also use these records to learn about the Earth itself.

For example, the fossil record helps paleontologists understand how Earth's climate and geography have changed. Fossils of plants that need a warm climate have been found in regions that, today, have a cold climate. That means the climate in that region changed a lot over the years!

Fossils can also tell scientists how Earth's continents have moved and changed. Similar fossils found on two separate continents tell us that, at one time, the continents were connected.

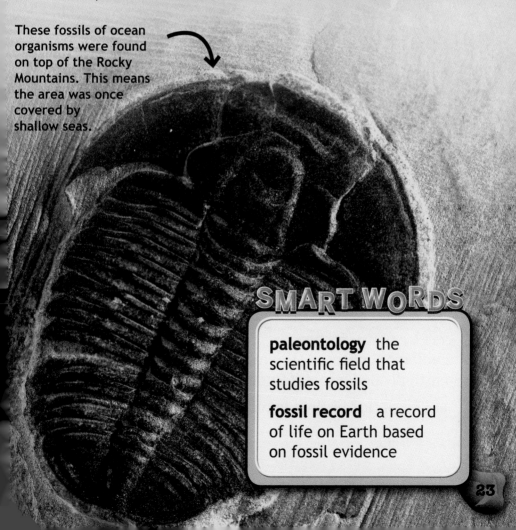

These fossils of ocean organisms were found on top of the Rocky Mountains. This means the area was once covered by shallow seas.

SMART WORDS

paleontology the scientific field that studies fossils

fossil record a record of life on Earth based on fossil evidence

Paleontologists also use the **geologic timescale** to study fossils. It divides the history of Earth into three big **eras**, or periods of time.

The Paleozoic Era is the earliest period. The next period is the Mesozoic Era. It is often called the Age of Dinosaurs. The third period is the Cenozoic Era. It is often called the Age of Mammals. We live in the Cenozoic Era today.

How do scientists know where a fossil belongs on the geologic timescale? Fossils are often found in sedimentary rock. New layers of rock form on top of old layers. Usually, deeper fossils are older than fossils above them. Scientists compare the layers and fossils to place them in the correct time period.

SMART WORDS

geologic timescale   the history of the Earth divided into different stages

era   a period of time in history

Era	Fossils	Time
Paleozoic	trilobite 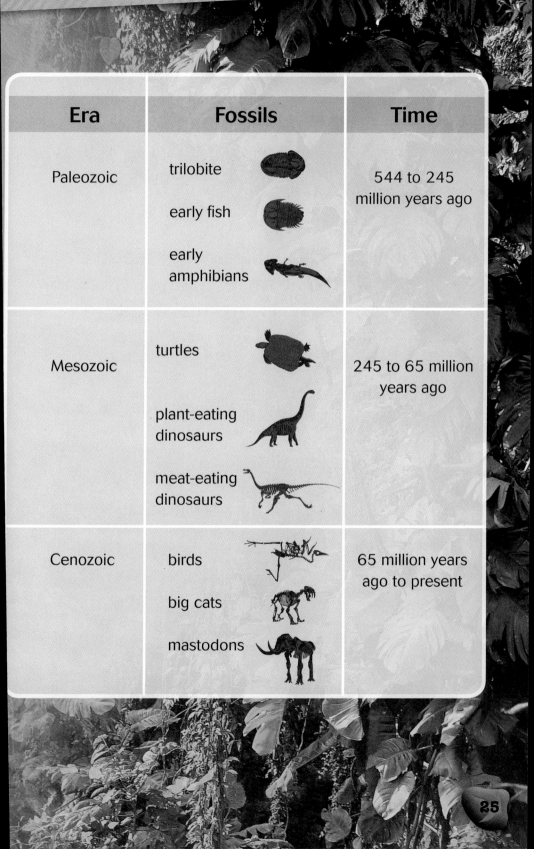 early fish early amphibians	544 to 245 million years ago
Mesozoic	turtles plant-eating dinosaurs meat-eating dinosaurs	245 to 65 million years ago
Cenozoic	birds big cats mastodons	65 million years ago to present

You do not have to be a paleontologist to collect fossils. You already know lots of new words that can help you get started. Now you just need a place to look. Good places to look are old quarries, beaches, or any cliffs along bodies of water.

Once you find a place to search, make sure you are allowed to be there. Always get permission to fossil hunt and make sure you have an adult with you.

If you find a fossil, follow these instructions:

- Take a photograph or make a note about the fossil before removing it.

- Wear safety goggles if you are chipping rocks.

- Use small hammers or brushes to remove materials around the fossil.

- Label the fossil with a description of the fossil.

Sue is a *T. rex*. It can be seen at the Field Museum in Chicago.

You may someday be as fortunate as Sue Hendrickson, a famous fossil hunter. In 1990, she found several *T. rex* bones in the hills of South Dakota. Then she dug up more and more.

Altogether, Sue Hendrickson dug up 200 dinosaur bones. They make up the largest *T. rex* skeleton ever found. Named after its discoverer, "Sue" is over 42 feet (13 meters) long.

Maybe one day you will find a fossil that writes another page in the story of Earth.

Answer each question with a Smart Word.

paleontology	geologic timescale
era	fossil record

1. What area of science studies fossils?

2. What is a record of life on Earth based on fossil evidence?

3. How would you describe a period of time in history?

4. What is the history of the Earth divided into different stages?

Answers on page 32

Talk Like a Scientist

Would you like to be a paleontologist? What kind of fossils would you like to study?

SMART FACTS

Did You Know?

Dinosaur National Monument is in Utah and Colorado. The rocks there contain amazing dinosaur fossils.

That's Amazing!

Some plants and animals have not changed over time. A gingko tree today looks just like a gingko tree did 20 million years ago.

Incredible Find!

One of the most famous fossil hunters was a girl named Mary Anning. She lived along the coast of England near sea cliffs full of fossils. In 1811, Mary discovered the complete fossil of an ichthyosaur, an ancient sea creature. Mary made this important discovery when she was only 12 years old.

This fossil is of an ichthyosaur. It had a fish-like body, four flippers, and a head like a dolphin.

Glossary

amber a hard substance made from the hardened sap of some evergreen trees

cast a fossil formed when sand, mud, or minerals harden inside a mold

era a period of time in history

evidence any sign or indication that proves something

extinct when all animals or plants of a certain type die and none are left

fossil any evidence or remains of an organism that once lived on Earth

fossil fuel fuel formed from the remains of ancient plants and animals

fossil record a record of life on Earth based on fossil evidence

geologic timescale the history of the Earth divided into different stages

imprint an impression left by a thin object in sand or mud that hardens into rock

mineral a nonliving solid that occurs in nature

mold a hollow space in the exact shape of the original organism

paleontology the scientific field that studies fossils

petrification the process in which an animal or plant turns to stone

preserve to protect something so that it stays in its original state

reproduce to make more of one's own kind

sediment small pieces of sand, mud, pebbles, and the remains of dead organisms

sedimentary rock rock formed by layers of sediment in the ground being pressed together

tar pit a pool of black, sticky tar

trace fossil a visible mark or sign of animal activity

Index

SMART WORDS Answer Key

Page 12
1. imprint, 2. trace fossil, 3. fossil, 4. cast, 5. mold,
6. extinct, 7. preserve, 8. evidence, 9. reproduce

Page 20
1. amber, 2. sedimentary rock, 3. petrification,
4. tar pit, 5. fossil fuel, 6. mineral, 7. sediment

Page 28
1. paleontology, 2. fossil record, 3. era,
4. geologic timescale